3 3052 09766 8752

I love reading

Dinosaur Babies

by Leonie Bennett

Consultant: Luis M. Chiappe, Ph.D.
Director of the Dinosaur Institute
Natural History Museum of Los Angeles County

BEARPORT
PUBLISHING

NEW YORK, NEW YORK

Credits

Cover, Title Page: Pulsar EStudio; 4, 6TR, 6BR, 8–9, 16: Simon Mendez; 5, 7, 12–13, 13TR, 17, 18, 19, 22, 24: Philip Hood; 6TL, 6BL, 23: Shutterstock; 10, 11, 20–21: Luis Rey; 13TL: Corbis; 14–15: Pulsar EStudio.

Every effort has been made by ticktock Entertainment Ltd. to trace copyright holders. We apologize in advance for any omissions. We would be pleased to insert the appropriate acknowledgments in any subsequent edition of this publication.

Library of Congress Cataloging-in-Publication Data

Bennett, Leonie.
Dinosaur babies / by Leonie Bennett.
   p. cm. — (I love reading. Dino world!)
Includes bibliographical references and index.
ISBN-13: 978-1-59716-544-0 (library binding)
ISBN-10: 1-59716-544-1 (library binding)
1. Dinosaurs—Infancy—Juvenile literature. 2. Dinosaurs—Juvenile literature. I. Title.

QE861.5.B4452 2008
567.9—dc22

2007017655

Contents

Dinosaur eggs 4

How big were dinosaur eggs?. 6

Laying eggs 8

Protecting their eggs 10

How big were dinosaur babies?. . . 12

Caring for babies 14

What did dinosaur babies eat?. . . . 16

A special dinosaur mother. 18

Sea babies 20

Glossary. 22

Index 24

Read More 24

Learn More Online. 24

Dinosaur eggs

Dinosaurs laid eggs.

Then the eggs **hatched**.

Baby dinosaurs came out of them.

Troodon eggs were **oval**.

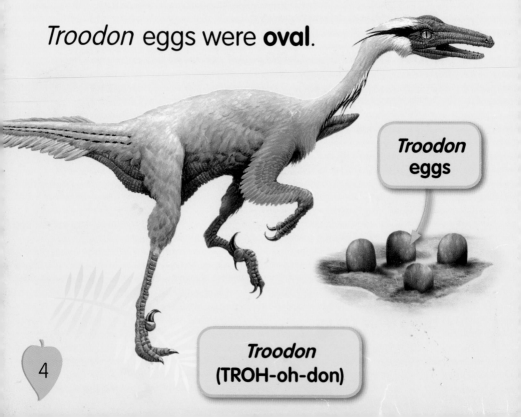

Troodon
eggs

Troodon
(TROH-oh-don)

Therizinosaurus eggs were round.

Therizinosaurus
(*ther*-uh-zeen-oh-SOR-uhss)

Therizinosaurus
egg

5

How big were dinosaur eggs?

Some eggs were bigger than a soccer ball.

Some eggs were smaller than a golf ball.

The biggest dinosaur egg found so far came from *Hypselosaurus.*

It was about 1 foot (30 cm) long.

Hypselosaurus
(*hip*-sel-oh-SOR-uhss)

Laying eggs

Some dinosaurs laid their eggs on top of the ground.

Other dinosaurs made nests for their eggs by digging holes in the ground.

eggs

Many sea creatures lived at the same time as dinosaurs.

Plesiosaurus lived in the sea.

However, it buried its eggs on the beach.

Plesiosaurus
(*plee*-zee-uh-**SOR**-uhss)

Protecting their eggs

Oviraptor sat on its nest to protect its eggs.

**Oviraptor
(oh-vih-RAP-tur)**

Big dinosaurs did not sit on their eggs.

They might break them!

Some big dinosaurs may have put leaves on their eggs to keep them warm.

How big were dinosaur babies?

One of the biggest dinosaurs was *Apatosaurus*.

A baby *Apatosaurus* was as big as a house cat.

An adult *Apatosaurus* could grow to 90 feet (27 m) long.

Apatosaurus
(uh-*pat*-uh-SOR-uhss)

A baby *Mussaurus* may be the smallest dinosaur **skeleton** ever found.

It was about 7 inches (17 cm) long.

Mussaurus
(moo-SOR-uhss)

Caring for babies

Some dinosaurs looked after
their babies.

This *Triceratops* mother is keeping her baby safe from a meat-eater.

Triceratops
(trye-SER-uh-tops)

What did dinosaur babies eat?

The babies of plant-eating dinosaurs ate leaves and twigs.

They had to learn to find the plants they could eat.

The babies of meat-eating dinosaurs ate meat.

They had to learn to **hunt**.

A special dinosaur mother

Maiasaura means "good mother lizard."

Maiasaura looked after her babies.

She fed them chewed-up plants.

Maiasaura
(*mye*-uh-SOR-uh)

19

Sea babies

All dinosaurs laid eggs.

Some sea creatures that lived at the same time as dinosaurs did not lay eggs.

Ichthyosaurus was a sea creature.

Its babies were born alive underwater.

Ichthyosaurus
(*ik*-thee-oh-SOR-uhss)

Glossary

hatched (HACHT)
when an animal
comes out of an egg

hunt (HUHNT)
to look for other
animals to eat

oval (OH-vuhl)
a shape like
an egg

skeleton (SKEL-uh-tuhn)
the framework of bones
that protect or support
the body

23

Index

Apatosaurus 12

Hypselosaurus 7

Ichthyosaurus 21

Maiasaura 18–19

Mussaurus 13

Oviraptor 10

Plesiosaurus 9

Therizinosaurus 5

Triceratops 15

Troodon 4

Read More

Lessem, Don. *Baby Dinosaurs (When Dinosaurs Lived).* New York: Grosset & Dunlap (2001).

Randall, Lee. *A Day in the Life of a Baby Dinosaur.* Mahwah, NJ: Troll Communications (1996).

Learn More Online

To learn more about the world of dinosaurs, visit
www.bearportpublishing.com/ILoveReading